746.46 ADA
Beyond neutral : quilts
inspired by nature's
elements
Adams, John Q., 1974-

Beyond Neu

QUILTS INSPIRED BY NATURE'S ELEMENTS

JOHN Q. ADAMS

Martingale
Create with Confidence

DEDICATION

For Megan, Bevin, and Sean, who inspire me to be creative and
be a better man every day. I love you with all my heart.

Beyond Neutral:
Quilts Inspired by Nature's Elements
© 2014 by John Q. Adams

Martingale®
19021 120th Ave. NE, Ste. 102
Bothell, WA 98011-9511 USA
ShopMartingale.com

No part of this product may be reproduced in any form,
unless otherwise stated, in which case reproduction
is limited to the use of the purchaser. The written
instructions, photographs, designs, projects, and
patterns are intended for the personal, noncommercial
use of the retail purchaser and are under federal
copyright laws; they are not to be reproduced by any
electronic, mechanical, or other means, including
informational storage or retrieval systems, for commercial
use. Permission is granted to photocopy patterns for the
personal use of the retail purchaser. Attention teachers:
Martingale encourages you to use this book for teaching,
subject to the restrictions stated above.

The information in this book is presented in good
faith, but no warranty is given nor results guaranteed.
Since Martingale has no control over choice of
materials or procedures, the company assumes no
responsibility for the use of this information.

Printed in China
19 18 17 16 15 14   8 7 6 5 4 3 2 1

Library of Congress Cataloging-in-Publication Data is
available upon request.

ISBN: 978-1-60468-390-5

MISSION STATEMENT

*Dedicated to providing quality products and service
to inspire creativity.*

CREDITS

PRESIDENT AND CEO: Tom Wierzbicki

EDITOR IN CHIEF: Mary V. Green

DESIGN DIRECTOR: Paula Schlosser

MANAGING EDITOR: Karen Costello Soltys

ACQUISITIONS EDITOR: Karen M. Burns

TECHNICAL EDITOR: Nancy Mahoney

COPY EDITOR: Marcy Heffernan

PRODUCTION MANAGER: Regina Girard

COVER AND INTERIOR DESIGNER: Adrienne Smitke

PHOTOGRAPHER: Brent Kane

ILLUSTRATOR: Lisa Lauch

CONTENTS

4 ◆ INTRODUCTION

WIND AND SKY

7 ◆ CAPE LOOKOUT

11 ◆ GLACIER BAY

15 ◆ CANYONLANDS

19 ◆ FOX RIVER

EARTH

25 ◆ HALF MOON BAY

29 ◆ RAVEN ROCK

33 ◆ KATMAI

WATER

39 ◆ PACIFIC CREST

43 ◆ CAYUCOS

LEAVES AND GRASS

49 ◆ TRITON COVE

53 ◆ FALLEN TIMBERS

57 ◆ CASCADIA

LAVA, CORAL, AND STONE

61 ◆ GLIMMERGLASS

65 ◆ PINNACLES

71 ◆ FIRE ISLAND

75 ◆ BIG THICKET

79 ◆ ACKNOWLEDGMENTS

80 ◆ ABOUT THE AUTHOR

Introduction

I didn't come to quilting through normal channels such as a long-held family tradition or by attending instructor-led quilting classes. Instead, I taught myself the craft by immersing myself in the online world of blogs and tutorials. Because of this, I often feel unencumbered by some of the more traditional practices of quilting.

I often get questions from other quilters about my approach to color selection, fabric combinations, and pattern design. In many cases, the quilters are apprehensive—scared, almost—to push themselves out of their comfort zone. Some quilters might fear combining prints and patterns from different fabric collections or types. Others might fear being asymmetrical or less than precise in the composition of their quilt blocks or quilt tops. But most often—and most surprising to me—is the fear of using anything other than white and cream as the neutral background for their quilts. I've had countless blog comments from quilters expressing their hesitation to consider other background colors to complement the printed fabrics in their quilt tops.

In this book, I created 16 original quilt patterns that do not use white or cream as the neutral background color. Instead, I wanted to share my own personal approach to selecting neutral backgrounds for my quilt projects.

I have come to see the colors of nature as the true neutrals in craft, art, and design. Sure there is a place for white and cream (and even black) fabrics to offset and showcase your quilt's printed designs. But would you be so quick to include brown or gray in that consideration set? How about green, or blue, or red? I realized that I often look to these natural tones to take the place of solids or neutrals when selecting clothes. If it works for our personal wardrobe, why wouldn't it work for quilt designs as well?

I've organized this book around these "natural neutrals". I call them my elements of modern quilting. Whether you prefer the green shades of leaves and grass, or the rich blue tones of the ocean, the browns of sand, earth, and bark, or the gorgeous reds of hot lava or cool coral, I encourage you to look around you at what nature has designed when composing your next quilt project.

Look past white. Leave cream for another project. Be bold in your fabric and color selection. You might never look back.

Happy sewing!
John

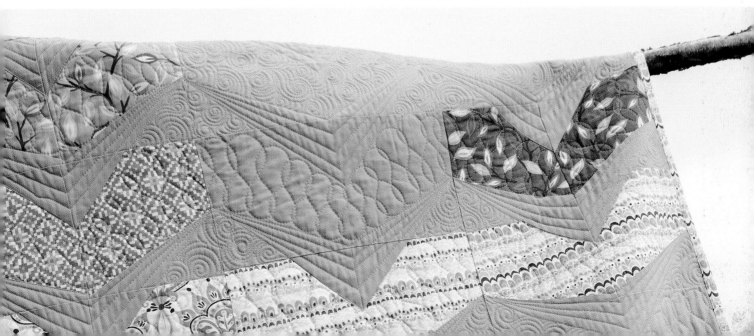

WIND AND SKY

♦ "Cape Lookout," pieced by John Q. Adams; quilted by Angela Walters.

Cape Lookout

I had been knocking around the idea for a quilt inspired by a land-scape at sunrise (or sunset) for quite a while, but was unsure how to realize it in patchwork form. I ultimately decided on a simple approach: columns of graduated squares and rectangles that, when cut and pieced from a favorite collection of nature-inspired prints, provide a perspective as if you were looking to the horizon. The solid vertical strips help to break up the prints, but are also reminiscent of gazing at this horizon through a gate or window.

For beginners, a quilt doesn't get much easier to piece. This is a wonderful pattern for the first-time quilter. I believe, however, that the quilt has appeal for quilters of all levels who might be looking for a quick project to showcase a favorite fabric line, to make a quick quilt to coordinate with the colors of a room, or as a go-to project for a gift quilt.

MATERIALS

Yardage is based on 42"-wide fabric. Fat quarters measure 18" x 21".

2 yards of dark-blue solid for background and sashing

⅓ yard *each* of 3 assorted prints (A–C)

¼ yard *each* of 3 assorted prints (D–F)

1 fat quarter *each* of 9 assorted prints (G–O)

⅔ yard of fabric for binding

5¼ yards of fabric for backing

80" x 88" piece of batting

Fabric Selections

Much of this quilt's beauty is derived from the careful selection and ordering of the focus fabrics. For my version of "Cape Lookout," I decided to select fabrics in the palette of a sunset and order them to create a gradated effect. To do so, I laid out my fabrics in the order I would sew them before cutting any of them. I carefully labeled them A–O starting from the bottom, so as not to lose track of their order. Whether you also decide on a gradated pattern, or an alternating or monochromatic one, I suggest you do the same and label your fabrics before cutting.

QUILT-TOP ASSEMBLY

1. To make the sashing strips, join two dark-blue 2½"-wide strips end to end to make a long strip. Press the seam allowances open. Make a total of eight long strips. Trim each long strip to measure 80½" long.

2. Join one rectangle or square of each assorted print in order from A to O along the 8½" edges to make a column. Add a dark-blue 8½" x 11½" rectangle to the fabric O rectangle to complete the column. Press the seam allowances in one direction (either toward the top or bottom of the column). Repeat to make seven identical columns.

CUTTING

From the dark-blue solid, cut:
2 strips, 11½" x 42"; cut into 7 rectangles, 8½" x 11½"
16 strips, 2½" x 42"

From *each* of fabrics A, B, and C, cut:
7 squares, 8½" x 8½" (21 total)

From *each* of fabrics D, E, and F, cut:
7 rectangles, 6½" x 8½" (21 total)

From *each* of fabrics G, H, and I, cut:
7 rectangles, 4½" x 8½" (21 total)

From *each* of fabrics, J, K, and L, cut:
7 rectangles, 3½" x 8½" (21 total)

From *each* of fabrics M, N, and O, cut:
7 rectangles, 2½" x 8½" (21 total)

From the binding fabric, cut:
8 strips, 2½" x 42"

Make 7.

Quilting details

3. Join the sashing strips and columns as shown in the quilt assembly diagram to complete the quilt top. Press the seam allowances toward the sashing strips. Trim and square up the quilt top as needed.

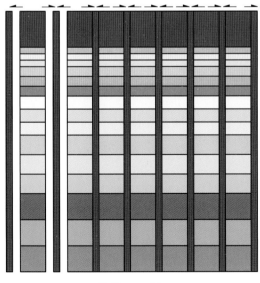

Quilt assembly

Aligning the Columns

When joining the columns and sashing strips, it's important for the seam lines to line up on each side of the sashing strip. One easy way to make sure the seams line up is to mark the strip with pins to show where the seams need to match. Then join the columns and sashing strips, matching the seam line with the pins.

FINISHING THE QUILT

For detailed instructions on finishing techniques, refer to ShopMartingale.com/HowtoQuilt.

1. Cut and piece the backing fabric so it is 6" to 8" larger than the quilt top. Layer the quilt top with batting and backing. Baste the layers together.

2. Hand or machine quilt as desired.

3. Square up the quilt sandwich.

4. Prepare and sew the binding to the quilt. Add a hanging sleeve, if desired, and a label.

◆ "Glacier Bay," pieced by Rosanne Derrett; quilted by Angela Walters.

Glacier Bay

FINISHED QUILT: 64½" x 76½" ◆ FINISHED BLOCK: 12" x 12"

"Glacier Bay" might be the most traditional pattern in this book. With this pattern, I wanted to design a 12" block and compose the quilt using only that block, laid out in a traditional way. Where I deviated from tradition, however, was in my selection of contemporary prints, my avoidance of typical block elements like stars and flying geese, and my choice of a bright, fresh color palette devoid of white and cream.

This quilt pattern is a great choice for a more traditional quilter who might be looking to venture into more modern territory, or for the modern quilter who might not usually make an entire quilt top from a single, repeated block.

Additionally, the versatility of the 12" block design makes this pattern great for sampler quilts, quilting bees, charity quilts, small projects, or other opportunities for which only a single block is needed.

MATERIALS

Yardage is based on 42"-wide fabric.

½ yard *each* of 10 assorted prints for blocks

2¼ yards of blue solid for blocks and border

⅔ yard of fabric for binding

5 yards of fabric for backing

72" x 84" piece of batting

CUTTING

From the blue solid, cut:
15 strips, 2½" x 42"; cut into 240 squares, 2½" x 2½"
5 strips, 3" x 42"; cut into 60 squares, 3" x 3"
8 strips, 2½" x 42"

From the assorted prints, cut a *total* of:
120 squares, 4½" x 4½" (30 sets of 4 matching squares)
120 rectangles, 2½" x 8½" (30 sets of 4 matching rectangles)*
60 squares, 3" x 3" (30 sets of 2 matching squares)*

From the binding fabric, cut:
8 strips, 2½" x 42"

The 30 sets of 3" squares should match the 30 sets of rectangles.

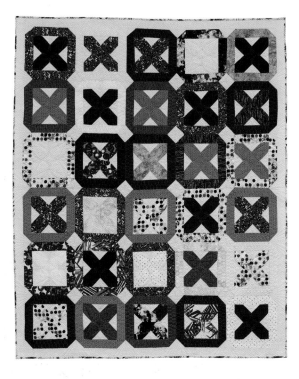

3. Lay out four matching units from step 2 in a four-patch arrangement, as shown below. Sew the units together into rows. Press the seam allowances in the directions indicated. Sew the rows together to complete a center unit. Press the seam allowances open. The unit should measure 8½" x 8½". Make a total of 30 units.

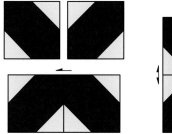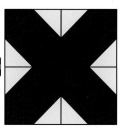

Make 30.

BLOCK ASSEMBLY

1. Draw a diagonal line from corner to corner on the wrong side of each blue 2½" square. Place a marked square on one corner of a print 4½" square, right sides together and raw edges aligned. Sew on the marked line. Trim the excess corner fabric, leaving a ¼" seam allowance, and press the resulting triangle open.

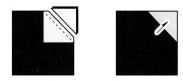

2. Repeat step 1, sewing a marked blue square on the opposite corner of the print square as shown. Make a total of 120 units in matching sets of four.

Make 120.

4. Draw a diagonal line from corner to corner on the wrong side of each blue 3" square. Layer a marked square right sides together with a print 3" square and stitch ¼" from each side of the marked line.

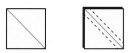

5. Cut the squares apart on the drawn line to create two half-square-triangle units. Press the seam allowances open. Trim each unit to measure 2½" square. Make a total of 120 half-square-triangle units.

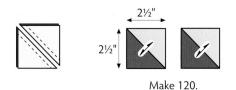

2½"

2½"

Make 120.

6. Lay out four half-square-triangle units and four print rectangles, all matching, and one center unit as shown. Sew the pieces together into rows. Press the seam allowances toward the rectangles. Join the rows to complete the block. Press the seam allowances toward the rectangles. The block should measure 12½" x 12½". Make a total of 30 blocks.

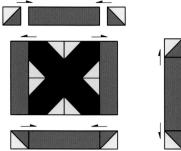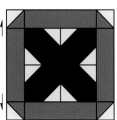

Make 30.

QUILT-TOP ASSEMBLY

1. Lay out the blocks in six rows of five blocks each as shown in the quilt assembly diagram at right, distributing your prints and colors in an eye-pleasing way. When you are pleased with the arrangement, sew the blocks together in rows. Press the seam allowances in opposite directions from row to row. Join the rows and press the seam allowances in one direction. The quilt top should measure 60½" x 72½".

2. Join two blue 2½"-wide strips end to end to make a long strip. Press the seam allowances open. Make a total of four long strips. Trim two long strips to measure 72½" long. Trim the remaining two long strips to measure 64½" long.

3. Sew the 72½"-long strips to the left and right sides of the quilt top. Press the seam allowances toward the border strips.

4. Sew the 64½"-long strips to the top and bottom of the quilt top to complete the border. Press the seam allowances toward the border strips.

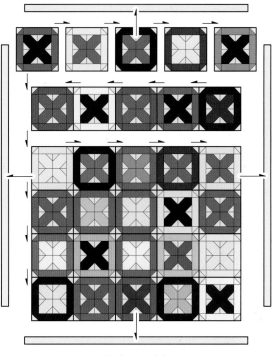

Quilt assembly

FINISHING THE QUILT

For detailed instructions on finishing techniques, refer to ShopMartingale.com/HowtoQuilt.

1. Cut and piece the backing fabric so it is 6" to 8" larger than the quilt top. Layer the quilt top with batting and backing. Baste the layers together.

2. Hand or machine quilt as desired.

3. Square up the quilt sandwich.

4. Prepare and sew the binding to the quilt. Add a hanging sleeve, if desired, and a label.

◆ "Canyonlands," pieced by John Q. Adams; quilted by Angela Walters.

Canyonlands

FINISHED QUILT: 60½" x 84½" • FINISHED BLOCK: 12" x 12"

A friend recently forwarded me a YouTube video of a "murmuration," the name for a flock of starlings flying in formation. It is truly a wonder of nature, and if you've never seen this phenomenon before, you should really check it out.

The video inspired me to actualize a quilt-block idea that had been forming in my head: an interpretation of birds in flight, abstract enough to result in a stunningly modern quilt. A Single Starling block finishes at 6" x 12", and a Double Starling block finishes at 12" square. The standard block size makes this an incredibly versatile quilt design, allowing for easy customization and resizing. It's also a pattern that would look just as lovely in a coordinated color palette as it would completely scrappy.

MATERIALS

Yardage is based on 42"-wide fabric. Fat quarters measure 18" x 21".

4½ yards of tan solid for blocks and quilt background

16 fat quarters *OR* ½ yard *each* of 8 different assorted prints for blocks

⅔ yard of fabric for binding

5⅜ yards of fabric for backing

68" x 92" piece of batting

CUTTING

From the *crosswise grain* of the tan solid, cut:
9 strips, 3½" x 42"; cut into 92 squares, 3½" x 3½"
6 strips, 9" x 42"; cut into 46 rectangles, 4½" x 9"

From the *lengthwise grain* of the remaining tan solid, cut:
1 strip, 12½" x 48½"
3 squares, 12½" x 12½"
10 rectangles, 6½" x 12½"

From the assorted prints, cut a *total* of:*
92 squares, 6½" x 6½"

From the binding fabric, cut:
8 strips, 2½" x 42"

You should be able to cut 6 squares from each fat quarter or 12 squares from each ½-yard cut.

BLOCK ASSEMBLY

This quilt is made of two different blocks, a Double Starling block and a Single Starling block.

Block A—Double Starling Block

1. Draw a diagonal line from corner to corner on the wrong side of two tan 3½" squares. Place a marked square on the upper-right corner of a print square, right sides together and raw edges aligned. Sew on the marked line. Trim the excess corner fabric, leaving a ¼" seam allowance, and press the resulting triangle open.

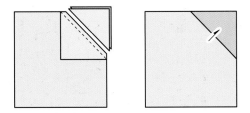

2. Along the left edge of the print square, measure 3" up from the bottom left corner and make a light pencil mark. Using a ruler, make a cut from this pencil mark to the bottom right corner of the square.

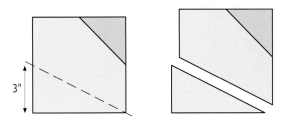

3. Cut a tan 4½" x 9" rectangle in half diagonally, from the top-left to the bottom-right corner.

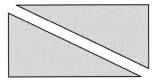

4. Sew one triangle from step 3 to the angled edge of the unit as shown. The triangle was cut a bit oversize for easier cutting and piecing. Press the seam allowances toward the tan triangle. Trim the unit to 6½" square.

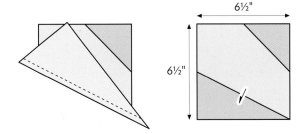

5. Repeat steps 1 and 2 to make the other half-block unit. Cut a tan 4½" x 9" rectangle in half diagonally, from the top-right to the bottom-left corner. Repeat step 4, sewing one triangle to the angled edge of the unit as shown to complete the unit. This unit is a mirror image of the first unit.

6. Lay out two mirror-image units made with the same print so that the print forms a V shape. Join the units to make a 6½" x 12½" starling unit. Press the seam allowances open. Repeat the steps to make a total of 36 units.

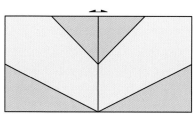

Make 36.

7. Join two starlings units to make block A. The block should measure 12½" x 12½". Press the seam allowances open. Make a total of 18 of block A.

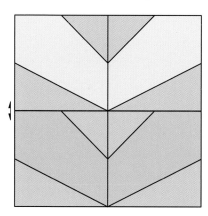

Block A.
Make 18.

Make It Scrappy

Consider varying your focus and background fabrics for scrappy Starling blocks.

Block B—Single Starling Block

1. Follow steps 1–6 of "Block A—Double Starling" to make a starling unit. Make 10 units.

2. Sew a tan 6½" x 12½" rectangle to the bottom of five of the units to make the B1 blocks. Press the seam allowances toward the tan rectangle.

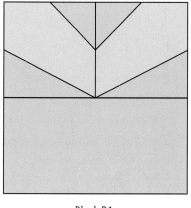

Block B1.
Make 5.

3. Sew a tan 6½" x 12½" rectangle to the top of each remaining starling unit to make five B2 blocks. Press the seam allowances toward the tan rectangle.

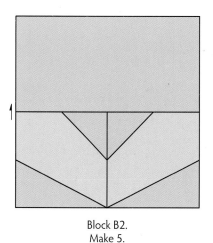

Block B2.
Make 5.

QUILT-TOP ASSEMBLY

1. Lay out the A, B1, and B2 blocks, along with the tan 12½" squares and tan 12½" x 48½" strip, as shown in the quilt assembly diagram below. Join the blocks into rows; press the seam allowances in opposite directions from row to row.

2. Join the rows to complete the quilt top. Press the seam allowances in one direction. Trim and square up the quilt top as needed.

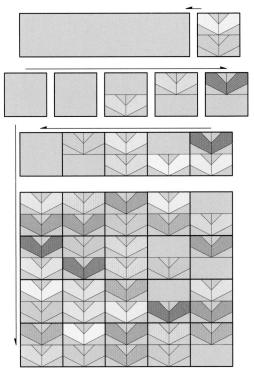

Quilt assembly

FINISHING THE QUILT

For detailed instructions on finishing techniques, refer to ShopMartingale.com/HowtoQuilt.

1. Cut and piece the backing fabric so it is 6" to 8" larger than the quilt top. Layer the quilt top with batting and backing. Baste the layers together.

2. Hand or machine quilt as desired.

3. Square up the quilt sandwich.

4. Prepare and sew the binding to the quilt. Add a hanging sleeve, if desired, and a label.

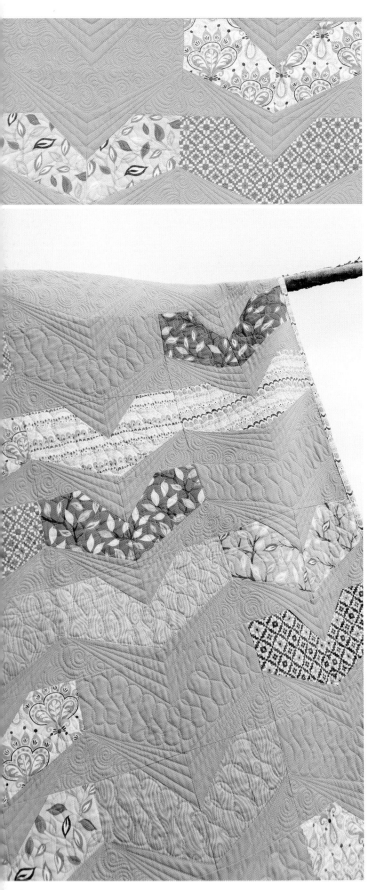

Quilting details

Fox River

FINISHED QUILT: 64½" x 71½" ◆ **FINISHED BLOCK: 8" x 8"**

For whatever reason, I have a bias toward designing my quilt patterns in columns. I tend to think through my quilts from top to bottom (or bottom to top), in visual flow as well as in preferred methods of construction. It must just be how I'm wired. For this quilt, I made a conscious decision to flip my ideas on their side and design a quilt in rows. I couldn't be happier with how it turned out.

The idea for the quilt began with the collection of prints starring foxes, owls, turtles, and other forest friends. I've found that quilters will often default to using browns and greens as their neutrals when pairing with woodland prints and, similarly, pair blues with nautical or beach-themed prints. For this quilt, I instead chose a turquoise blue as the backdrop for the woodland creatures and woodgrain prints of the fabrics. I love the lighter, more whimsical tone that the choice achieved.

MATERIALS

Yardage is based on 42"-wide fabric. Fat quarters measure 18" x 21".

16 fat quarters of assorted prints for blocks

1 yard of turquoise solid for blocks and sashing

⅝ yard of fabric for binding

4½ yards of fabric for backing

72" x 79" piece of batting

CUTTING

From the turquoise solid, cut:
7 strips, 2" x 42"; cut into 128 squares, 2" x 2"
12 strips, 1½" x 42"

From *each* print, cut:
8 rectangles, 4½" x 8½" (128 total)*

From the binding fabric, cut:
7 strips, 2½" x 42"

*The rectangles in the quilt are oriented vertically. If using a directional fabric, you'll want to cut your rectangles accordingly.

◆ "Fox River," pieced by Carol Lane Fleming; quilted by Angela Walters.

BLOCK ASSEMBLY

1. Draw a diagonal line from corner to corner on the wrong side of each turquoise square. Place a marked square on one corner of print rectangle, right sides together. Sew on the marked line. Trim the excess corner fabric, leaving a ¼" seam allowance, and press the resulting triangle open. Repeat to make a mirror-image unit. Make 64 of each unit (128 total).

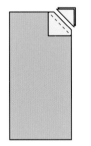

Make 64 of each.

Taking Control

If you're using directional prints, refer to the quilt assembly diagram on page 22 to determine which corner to cover. You'll place the marked square on the top-right corner of 32 rectangles, the bottom-right corner of 32 rectangles, the top-left corner of 32 rectangles, and the bottom-left corner of 32 rectangles. You may want to lay out all of the rectangles on your floor or design wall first.

2. Sew two mirror-image units with matching fabrics together as shown to make a block. Press the seam allowances open. Make a total of 56 blocks. You'll have 16 units left over to use when assembling the block rows.

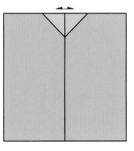

Make 56.

QUILT-TOP ASSEMBLY

1. Join the turquoise 1½"-wide strips end to end. Press the seam allowances open. From the pieced strip, cut seven 64½"-long sashing strips.

2. Lay out the blocks in eight rows of seven blocks each, rotating the blocks as shown in the quilt assembly diagram on page 22. Place a rectangular unit at both ends of each row, rotating the units as shown. Join the blocks and units into rows. Press the seam allowances open.

3. Sew the block rows and seven sashing strips together, alternating them as shown. Press the seam allowances toward the sashing strips. Trim and square up the quilt top as needed.

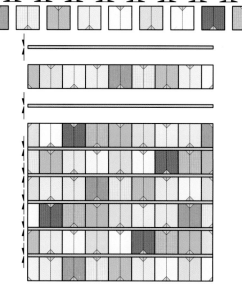

Quilt assembly

FINISHING THE QUILT

For detailed instructions on finishing techniques, refer to ShopMartingale.com/HowtoQuilt.

1. Cut and piece the backing fabric so it is 6" to 8" larger than the quilt top. Layer the quilt top with batting and backing. Baste the layers together.

2. Hand or machine quilt as desired.

3. Square up the quilt sandwich.

4. Prepare and sew the binding to the quilt. Add a hanging sleeve, if desired, and a label.

Quilting details

EARTH

◆ "Half Moon Bay," pieced by Kristen Danis; quilted by Angela Walters.

Half Moon Bay

FINISHED QUILT: 62½" x 82½" ◆ FINISHED BLOCK: 8" x 8"

Sometimes the simplest quilt patterns can have the most impact. Take this quilt as an example. The blocks are easily constructed from basic squares and rectangles and the quilt assembly is uncomplicated. But when all of these elements are put together, the end result makes a big statement.

I can see many things in this quilt, starting with abstract flower petals. Vertical and horizontal movement pulls my eye back and forth and up and down the quilt. The offset diamond pattern lends a structured and geometric feel. All of these aspects are achieved by a pattern that, at its core, is quite simple.

For this quilt, I took my inspiration from beach-themed prints containing algae, coral, and shells washed up on the shore. Though watery blue or sandy beige would be the obvious neutral background to achieve this feel, I instead went with a deep, dark brown. I really like the drama that the dark solid added to the quilt, serving to both highlight the prints and evoke the feeling of trees and bark in a beachside glen.

MATERIALS

Yardage is based on 42"-wide fabric. Fat quarters measure 18" x 21".

12 fat quarters of assorted prints for blocks

2⅝ yards of dark-brown solid for blocks, sashing, and border

⅔ yard of fabric for binding

5¼ yards of fabric for backing

70" x 90" piece of batting

CUTTING

From the dark-brown solid, cut:
24 strips, 2½" x 42"; cut 6 *of the strips* into 96 squares, 2½" x 2½"
3 strips, 8½" x 42"; cut into 42 strips, 2½" x 8½"

From *each* fat quarter, cut:
8 rectangles, 4½" x 8½" (96 total)

From the binding fabric, cut:
8 strips, 2½" x 42"

BLOCK ASSEMBLY

1. Draw a diagonal line from corner to corner on the wrong side of each dark-brown 2½" square. Place a marked square on one corner of a print 4½" x 8½" rectangle. Sew along the marked line and trim away the corner fabric, leaving a ¼" seam allowance. Press the resulting triangle open. Repeat to make a mirror-image unit. Make 48 of each unit (96 total).

Make 48 of each.

Working with Directional Prints

If you're using directional prints, refer to the quilt assembly diagram on page 27 to determine which corner of the print rectangle to cover. You may want to place all of the rectangles on your floor or design wall to make sure they are oriented correctly before sewing any of the units.

2. Lay out two units from step 1 with the dark-brown triangles in the upper-right and bottom-left corners as shown. Sew the units together along the long edges to complete a block. Press the seam allowances toward the darker rectangle. Make 24 of block A.

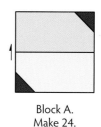

Block A.
Make 24.

3. Lay out two units from step 1 with the dark-brown triangles in the upper-left and lower-right corners as shown. Sew the units together along the long edges to complete a block. Press the seam allowances toward the darker rectangle. Make 24 of block B.

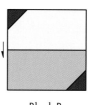

Block B.
Make 24.

QUILT-TOP ASSEMBLY

1. Join two dark-brown 2½" x 42" strips end to end to make a long strip. Press the seam allowances open. Make a total of nine long strips. Trim seven of the long strips to measure 78½" long each. Trim the remaining two long strips to each measure 62½" long.

2. Referring to the quilt assembly diagram on page 27 for placement guidance, lay out four A blocks, four B blocks, and seven dark-brown 2½" x 8½" sashing strips each in six vertical columns, alternating the blocks and sashing strips as shown. Sew the blocks and strips together to make columns. Press the seam allowances toward the strips. The columns should measure 78½" long.

Quilting details

3. Sew the block columns and the 78½"-long pieced strips together, alternating them as shown in the assembly diagram at right. Press the seam allowances toward the sashing strips.

4. Sew the 62½"-long pieced strips to the top and bottom edges to complete the quilt top. Press the seam allowances toward the strips.

FINISHING THE QUILT

For detailed instructions on finishing techniques, refer to ShopMartingale.com/HowtoQuilt.

1. Cut and piece the backing fabric so it is 6" to 8" larger than the quilt top. Layer the quilt top with batting and backing. Baste the layers together.

2. Hand or machine quilt as desired.

3. Square up the quilt sandwich.

4. Prepare and sew the binding to the quilt. Add a hanging sleeve, if desired, and a label.

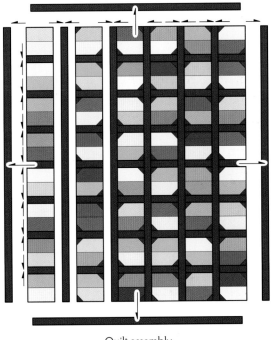

Quilt assembly

♦ "Raven Rock," pieced by John Q. Adams; quilted by Angela Walters.

Raven Rock

This modern quilt, a variation of a simple strip quilt made from squares, rectangles, and triangles, creates an interesting visual effect that evokes movement (or shifting) due to the deliberate placement of its prints and colors. I designed this quilt both to showcase large prints and to emphasize a favorite color and pattern combination. As I was drawing plans for this quilt, it also seemed to represent a somewhat abstract interpretation of a tree trunk.

MATERIALS

Yardage is based on 42"-wide fabric. Because long continuous strips, cut from the lengthwise grain, are required for this quilt, more yardage is required than you'll actually use when piecing the quilt top. If you're using a favorite color or print, there should be plenty of leftover fabric for additional projects—either another quilt, or maybe some coordinating pillows or shams. Another suggestion is to use the leftover fabrics to make a pieced back instead of purchasing backing fabric. If you prefer a more efficient use of fabric, you can use strips cut across the grain of the fabric and piece the long strips, which will require less yardage.

You'll need 10 fabrics for the quilt top, arranged in order from left to right as A through J.

2⅛ yards of fabric A

1¾ yards of fabric B

1¾ yards of fabric C

1⅝ yards of fabric D

1⅛ yards of fabric E

1⅝ yards of fabric F

2 yards of fabric G

2 yards of fabric H

½ yard of fabric I

½ yard of fabric J

¾ yard of fabric for binding

7½ yards of fabric for backing

88" x 94" piece of batting

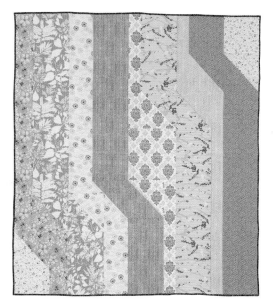

CUTTING

If using directional prints, be sure to refer to the quilt assembly diagram on page 32 before making any cuts, especially when cutting a square in half diagonally. This will ensure that your pieces can be placed in such a way as to keep the orientation of the print intact.

From fabric A, cut:
1 strip, 6½" x 68½" (A1)
1 square, 13" x 13"; cut in half diagonally to yield
  2 triangles (A2, A3)
1 strip, 6½" x 20½" (A4)

From the *lengthwise grain* of fabric B, cut:
1 strip, 12½" x 56½" (B1)
1 square, 13" x 13"; cut in half diagonally to yield
  2 triangles (B2, B3)
1 strip, 12½" x 20½" (B4)

From the *lengthwise grain* of fabric C, cut:
1 strip, 8½" x 56½" (C1)
1 square, 13" x 13"; cut in half diagonally to yield
  2 triangles (C2; 1 triangle is extra)
1 square, 5" x 5"; cut in half diagonally to yield
  2 triangles (C3; 1 triangle is extra)
1 square, 9" x 9"; cut in half diagonally to yield
  2 triangles (C4; 1 triangle is extra)
1 strip, 8½" x 24½" (C5)

From the *lengthwise grain* of fabric D, cut:
1 strip, 12½" x 52½" (D1)
1 square, 5" x 5"; cut in half diagonally to yield
  2 triangles (D2; 1 triangle is extra)
1 rectangle, 4½" x 8½" (D3)
1 square, 9" x 9"; cut in half diagonally to yield
  2 triangles (D4; 1 triangle is extra)
1 square, 13" x 13"; cut in half diagonally to yield
  2 triangles (D5; 1 triangle is extra)
1 strip, 12½" x 24½" (D6)

From fabric E, cut:
2 strips, 4½" x 36½" (E1, E5)
1 square, 13" x 13"; cut in half diagonally to yield
  2 triangles (E2, E3)
1 square, 16½" x 16½" (E4)

From the *lengthwise grain* of fabric F, cut:
1 strip, 12½" x 24½" (F1)
1 square, 13" x 13"; cut in half diagonally to yield
  2 triangles (F2, F3)
1 strip, 12½" x 52½" (F4)

From the *lengthwise grain* of fabric G, cut:
1 strip, 4½" x 24½" (G1)
1 square, 13" x 13"; cut in half diagonally to yield
  2 triangles (G2, G3)
1 strip, 4½" x 64½" (G4)

From the *lengthwise grain* of fabric H, cut:
1 square, 12½" x 12½" (H1)
1 square, 13" x 13"; cut in half diagonally to yield
  2 triangles (H2, H3)
1 strip, 12½" x 64½" (H4)

From fabric I, cut:
1 square, 12½" x 12½" (I1)
1 square, 13" x 13"; cut in half diagonally to yield
  2 triangles (I2; 1 triangle is extra)

From fabric J, cut:
1 square, 13" x 13"; cut in half diagonally to yield
  2 triangles (J1; 1 triangle is extra)
1 rectangle, 8½" x 12½" (J2)

From the binding fabric, cut:
9 strips, 2½" x 42"

Quilting details

QUILT-TOP ASSEMBLY

This quilt is easily assembled in five vertical rows or columns. Before starting to sew, I recommend laying out all the pieces on the floor or on your design wall according to the assembly diagram on page 32. After sewing each seam, return the completed unit or row to its correct position in the quilt layout.

1. Sew the A2 and J1 triangles together along their long edges to make a half-square-triangle unit. Press the seam allowances to one side (or press them open). Trim the unit to measure 12½" x 12½".

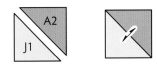

2. Repeat step 1 to make half-square-triangle units for each color combination as follows:

   - Join A3 and B2 triangles. Trim to 12½" x 12½".
   - Join B3 and C2 triangles. Trim to 12½" x 12½".
   - Join C3 and D2 triangles. Trim to 4½" x 4½".
   - Join C4 and D4 triangles. Trim to 8½" x 8½".
   - Join D5 and E3 triangles. Trim to 12½" x 12½".

   - Join E2 and F2 triangles. Trim to 12½" x 12½".
   - Join F3 and G3 triangles. Trim to 12½" x 12½".
   - Join G2 and H2 triangles. Trim to 12½" x 12½".
   - Join H3 and I2 triangles. Trim to 12½" x 12½".

3. For row 1, sew the A3/B2 unit to the bottom edge of the B1 strip. Then sew the A1 strip to the left edge of the strip to make the top section. Sew the J1/A2 unit to the J2 rectangle; then add the A4 strip to the right edge to make the bottom section. Join the two sections to complete row 1. Press the seam allowances in the directions indicated in the assembly diagram on page 32.

4. For row 2, sew the C3/D2 unit to the D3 rectangle. Then add the D1 strip to the top edge. Sew the C1 strip to the left edge to make the top section. Join the B3/C2 unit to the B4 strip. Join the C4/D4 unit to the C5 strip. Join the two strips to make the bottom section. Join the two sections to complete row 2. Press the seam allowances in the directions indicated.

5. For row 3, sew the E2/F2 unit to the F1 strip. Then add the E1 strip to the left edge and the E4 square to the bottom edge to make the top section. Join the D5/E3 unit to the

D6 strip. Then add the E5 strip to make the bottom section. Join the two sections to complete row 3. Press the seam allowances in the directions indicated.

6. For row 4, sew the G2/H2 unit to the H1 square; add the G1 strip to make the top section. Sew the F3/G3 unit to the F4 strip; then add the G4 strip to make the bottom section. Join the two sections to complete row 4. Press the seam allowances in the directions indicated.

7. For row 5, sew the H3/I2 unit to the I1 square; add the H4 strip to the bottom edge to complete the row; press.

8. Join the five vertical rows to complete the quilt top. Press the seam allowances open.

FINISHING THE QUILT

For detailed instructions on finishing techniques, refer to ShopMartingale.com/HowtoQuilt.

1. Cut and piece the backing fabric so it is 6" to 8" larger than the quilt top. Layer the quilt top with batting and backing. Baste the layers together.

2. Hand or machine quilt as desired.

3. Square up the quilt sandwich.

4. Prepare and sew the binding to the quilt. Add a hanging sleeve, if desired, and a label.

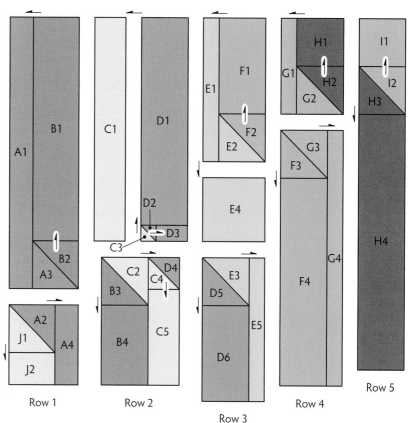

Quilt assembly

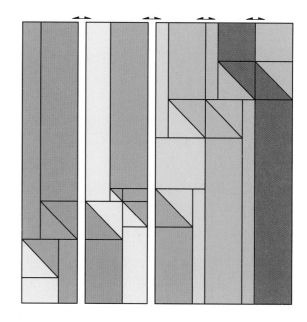

Katmai

This quilt was born out of my attempt at designing a more traditional quilt block—not a whole quilt top, but simply a block. I figured if I could put my own spin on a single block and make a whole quilt from that block, it would be a nice addition to this collection.

But a strange thing happened. As I started to sketch the block on graph paper, adding layers and borders of squares, rectangles, and flying geese, the block started getting bigger. And bigger. And by the time I was happy with the overall design of the block, the block itself was 32" square. That's a BIG block.

Now sure, I could have scaled the whole thing down to a more typically sized block, but I had an amazing collection of fabric that featured large-scale prints of bears, birds, and woodgrains. I didn't want to lose any of the prints by cutting them down too small. Besides, I kind of fell in love with the idea of a 32" block.

The final quilt comprises four blocks, laid out in a two-by-two grid with top and bottom borders to add length. But the potential to make this quilt many different ways—with different colors, layouts, combinations of patterns and textures, and by playing with coordinating (or not coordinating) the four blocks—is exciting.

MATERIALS

Yardage is based on 42"-wide fabric.

3⅛ yards of brown solid for blocks and border

⅝ yard *each* of 4 assorted dark prints for blocks

⅝ yard *total* of 2 woodgrain prints for blocks

⅞ yard *each* of 2 assorted light prints for blocks

⅔ yard of fabric for binding

4½ yards of fabric for backing

72" x 80" piece of batting

CUTTING

From the brown solid, cut:
22 strips, 4½" x 42"; cut *18 of the strips* into:
    32 rectangles, 4½" x 8½"
    80 squares, 4½" x 4½"

From *each* of the assorted dark prints, cut:
5 squares, 8½" x 8½" (20 total)

From the woodgrain prints, cut a *total* of:
2 strips, 8½" x 42"; cut into 16 rectangles,
    4½" x 8½" (4 sets of 4 matching rectangles.)

From *each* assorted light print, cut:
6 strips, 4½" x 42"; cut into:
    16 squares, 4½" x 4½" (32 total)
    16 rectangles, 4½" x 8½" (32 total)

From the binding fabric, cut:
8 strips, 2½" x 42"

◆ "Katmai," pieced by Cathy Reitan; quilted by Angela Walters.

Quilting details

BLOCK ASSEMBLY

1. Draw a diagonal line from corner to corner on the wrong side of each brown square. Place a marked square on one end of a light rectangle, right sides together. Sew on the marked line. Trim the excess corner fabric, leaving a ¼" seam allowance, and press the resulting triangle open. Repeat the process on the other end of the rectangle to complete a flying-geese unit. Make a total of 32 units.

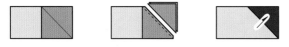

Make 32.

Chain Piecing

Chain piecing is a quick and effective way to make these units!

2. Repeat step 1 using two light squares and one brown rectangle. Make a total of 16 of these units.

Make 16.

3. Refer to the photo on page 34 and the quilt assembly diagram on page 36 for placement guidance. Lay out eight units from step 1, four units from step 2, four brown squares, four brown rectangles, four woodgrain rectangles, and five dark 8½" squares as shown. Join the pieces into rows and press the seam allowances in the directions indicated. Join the rows to complete one block. Press the seam allowances toward the center. The block should measure 32½" square. Make a total of four blocks.

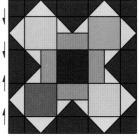

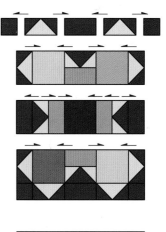

Make 4.

QUILT-TOP ASSEMBLY

1. Arrange the blocks in two rows of two blocks each, distributing your prints and colors as desired. When you are pleased with the arrangement, sew the blocks together into rows. Press the seam allowances in the opposite direction from row to row. Join the blocks and press the seam allowances in one direction.

2. Sew two brown 4½" x 42" strips together end to end. Press the seam allowances open. Trim the pieced strip to measure 64½" long. Repeat to make a second 64½"-long pieced strip.

3. Sew the pieced strips to the top and bottom of the quilt top. Press the seam allowances toward the strips. Trim and square up the quilt top as needed.

FINISHING THE QUILT

For detailed instructions on finishing techniques, refer to ShopMartingale.com/HowtoQuilt.

1. Cut and piece the backing fabric so it is 6" to 8" larger than the quilt top. Layer the quilt top with batting and backing. Baste the layers together.

2. Hand or machine quilt as desired.

3. Square up the quilt sandwich.

4. Prepare and sew the binding to the quilt. Add a hanging sleeve, if desired, and a label.

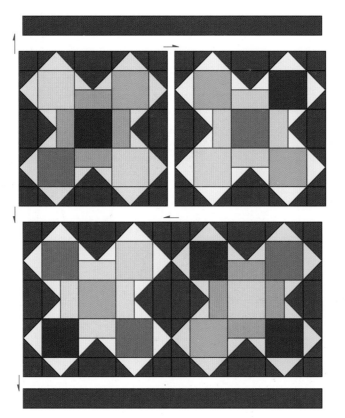

Quilt assembly

WATER

◆ "Pacific Crest," pieced by Melinda "Meli" Mathis; quilted by Angela Walters.

Pacific Crest

FINISHED QUILT: 72½" x 84½" ◆ FINISHED BLOCK: 12" x 12"

I'm just going to say it: navy blue is the most underrated crayon in the crayon box. I think this holds true for quilters and their willingness to look to this versatile color for their quilt projects, especially as the backdrop upon which they build their fabric palette. You need only take one look in my closet to see that I've always been a big fan of navy blue in the clothes I wear, so why shouldn't it be equally loved in the quilts that I make? Dark blue can help make stars of other colors in your quilt projects. Orange, red, yellow, and even lighter shades of blue really come to life when contrasted with deeper shades of navy and indigo.

The fabric collection I used in this quilt was the perfect choice to be paired with navy blue. With the colors and prints selected, I drew inspiration for the quilt pattern from the image of the flying cranes in one of the prints. I interpreted the flying birds into a collection of winged blocks in two sizes, laid out in an asymmetrical repeat to mimic the movement of a flock of birds, both from close and far away vantage points.

MATERIALS

Yardage is based on 42"-wide fabric. Fat quarters measure 18" x 21".

4½ yards of navy solid for background

½ yard *each* of 4 assorted prints for block A

7 fat quarters of assorted prints for block B

¾ yard of fabric for binding

5⅜ yards of fabric for backing

80" x 92" piece of batting

CUTTING

From the navy solid, cut:
4 strips, 7" x 42"; cut into 17 squares, 7" x 7"
8 strips, 6½" x 42"; cut into 45 squares, 6½" x 6½"
6 strips, 4" x 42"; cut into 52 squares, 4" x 4"
5 strips, 3½" x 42"; cut into 52 squares, 3½" x 3½"
2 strips, 12½" x 42"; cut into 5 squares, 12½" x 12½"

From *1* of the assorted prints for block A, cut:
5 squares, 7" x 7"
5 squares, 6½" x 6½"

From *each* of the remaining assorted prints for block A, cut:
4 squares, 7" x 7" (12 total)
4 squares, 6½" x 6½" (12 total)

From *each* of the assorted prints for block B, cut:
8 squares, 4" x 4" (56 total, 4 are extra)
8 squares, 3½" x 3½" (56 total, 4 are extra)

From the binding fabric, cut:
9 strips, 2½" x 42"

3. Lay out the half-square-triangle units, a matching print 6½" square, and a navy 6½" square in a four-patch arrangement as shown. Sew the pieces together into rows. Press the seam allowances toward the squares. Join the rows and press the seam allowances in one direction. Repeat the steps to make a total of 17 of block A.

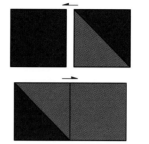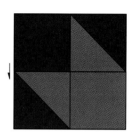

Block A.
Make 17.

BLOCK ASSEMBLY

This quilt top is made from three different block variations, blocks A, B, and C.

Block A

1. Draw a diagonal line from corner to corner on the wrong side of a navy 7" square. Layer the marked square right sides together with a print 7" square and stitch ¼" from each side of the marked line.

2. Cut the squares apart on the drawn line to create two half-square-triangle units. Press the seam allowances open. Trim each unit to measure 6½" square.

Block B

1. Repeat steps 1 and 2 of "Block A" using the navy and print 4" squares to make 104 half-square-triangle units. Trim each unit to measure 3½" square.

Make 104.

2. Lay out two half-square-triangle units, a matching print 3½" square, and a navy 3½" square in a four-patch arrangement as shown. Sew the pieces together into rows. Press the seam allowances toward the squares. Join the rows and press the seam allowances in one direction. Make a total of 52 units.

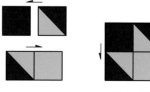

Make 52.

3. Lay out three units from step 2 and one navy 6½" square in a four-patch arrangement as shown. Sew the pieces together into rows. Press the seam allowances in the directions indicated. Join the rows and press. Make a total of three B1 blocks.

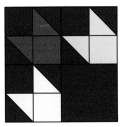

Block B1.
Make 3.

4. Repeat step 3 to make three B2 blocks, four B3 blocks, and two B4 blocks, making sure to orient the pieces as shown.

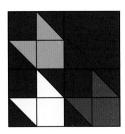

Block B2.
Make 3.

Block B3.
Make 4.

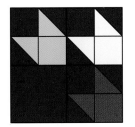

Block B4.
Make 2.

Block C

1. Lay out two navy 6½" squares and two units from step 2 of "Block B" in a four-patch arrangement as shown. Sew the pieces together into rows. Press the seam allowances in the directions indicated. Join the rows and press. Make a total of three C1 blocks.

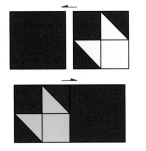
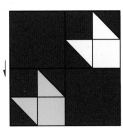

Block C1.
Make 3.

2. Repeat step 1 to make two C2 blocks, two C3 blocks, and one C4 block, making sure to orient the pieces as shown.

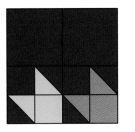

Block C2.
Make 2.

Block C3.
Make 2.

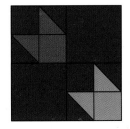

Block C4.
Make 1.

Quilting details

QUILT-TOP ASSEMBLY

1. Lay out the blocks and navy 12½" squares in seven rows of six pieces each, as shown in the quilt assembly diagram below, distributing your prints and colors as desired.

2. When you are pleased with the arrangement, sew the blocks together in rows. Press the seam allowances in opposite directions from row to row. Join the rows and press the seam allowances in one direction. Trim and square up the quilt top as needed.

FINISHING THE QUILT

For detailed instructions on finishing techniques, refer to ShopMartingale.com/HowtoQuilt.

1. Cut and piece the backing fabric so it is 6" to 8" larger than the quilt top. Layer the quilt top with batting and backing. Baste the layers together.

2. Hand or machine quilt as desired.

3. Square up the quilt sandwich.

4. Prepare and sew the binding to the quilt. Add a hanging sleeve, if desired, and a label.

Quilt assembly

Cayucos

FINISHED QUILT: 72½" x 82½" ◆ FINISHED BLOCK: 4" x 8"

Sometimes a good quilt design simply springs from working with your favorite fabrics and colors. That's precisely how this quilt came about. Eager to work with a long-hoarded fabric collection, I began thinking of ways to really bring the fabrics to life. At the same time, I was admiring all kinds of zigzag quilts and wondering how to create the movement that they effectively achieve, but in a new and different way.

My approach to the zigzag quilt brought together several elements: the use of patchwork squares; generous amounts of negative space to highlight the blue solid chosen for the quilt; an easy approach to assembling the quilt top in rows; and a design that achieves a three-dimensional perspective with all of the movement that I enjoyed in zigzag quilts.

Most of all, I am excited by the versatility of this quilt design. I think it would be stunning made with all solids, or with different styles of prints, or even by using a solid color other than blue to bring the negative space to life. The possibilities are infinite.

MATERIALS

Yardage is based on 42"-wide fabric. Fat quarters measure 18" x 21".

5 yards of blue solid for blocks and sashing

13 fat quarters of assorted prints for blocks

⅔ yard of fabric for binding

5¼ yards of fabric for backing

80" x 90" piece of batting

CUTTING

From the blue solid, cut:
26 strips, 4½" x 42"; cut into:
    128 squares, 4½" x 4½"
    40 rectangles, 4½" x 8½"
    18 strips, 2½" x 42"

From the assorted prints, cut a *total* of:
80 squares, 4½" x 4½"
64 rectangles, 4½" x 8½" *

From the binding fabric, cut:
7 strips, 2½" x 42"

*If you are using a directional fabric, be sure you cut the rectangles so that they are oriented vertically.

● "Cayucos," pieced by Rebecca Makas; quilted by Angela Walters.

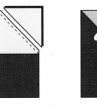

leaving a ¼" seam allowance, and press the resulting triangle open.

2. Place a marked square on the opposite end of the unit from step 1 as shown. Sew on the marked line. Trim the excess corner fabric, leaving a ¼" seam allowance, and press the resulting triangle open. Make 32 units.

Make 32.

3. Repeat steps 1 and 2 to make a mirror-image unit as shown. Make 32 units.

Make 32.

BLOCK A ASSEMBLY

Lay out two print squares and one blue rectangle as shown. Join the squares and press the seam allowances toward the darker square. Sew the rectangle to the squares to complete the block. Press the seam allowances toward the blue rectangle. The block should measure 8½" x 8½". Make a total of 40 of block A.

4. Join one unit from step 2 and one unit from step 3 as shown to complete the block. The block should measure 8½" x 8½". Press the seam allowances open. Make a total of 32 of block B.

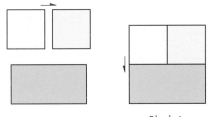

Block A.
Make 40.

BLOCK B ASSEMBLY

1. Draw a diagonal line from corner to corner on the wrong side of each blue square. Place a marked square on one end of print rectangle, right sides together, as shown. Sew on the marked line. Trim the excess corner fabric,

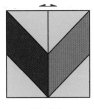

Block B.
Make 32.

Quilting details

QUILT-TOP ASSEMBLY

1. To make the sashing strips, join two 2½"-wide blue strips end to end to make a long strip. Press the seam allowances open. Make a total of nine long strips. Trim each long strip to measure 72½" long.

2. Sew five A blocks and four B blocks together as shown in the quilt assembly diagram below to make a block row. Press the seam allowances in one direction. The row should measure 72½" long. Make eight rows.

3. Sew the block rows and long sashing strips together, alternating them as shown in the quilt assembly diagram. Press the seam allowances toward the sashing strips. Trim and square up the quilt top as needed.

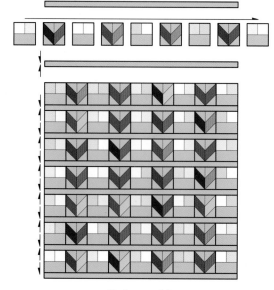

Quilt assembly

Alternating Seams

Each sashing strip will have a vertical seam where the two pieces were joined. Rotate the strip on every other row to alternate the placement of the joining seams.

FINISHING THE QUILT

For detailed instructions on finishing techniques, refer to ShopMartingale.com/HowtoQuilt.

1. Cut and piece the backing fabric so it is 6" to 8" larger than the quilt top. Layer the quilt top with batting and backing. Baste the layers together.

2. Hand or machine quilt as desired.

3. Square up the quilt sandwich.

4. Prepare and sew the binding to the quilt. Add a hanging sleeve, if desired, and a label.

LEAVES AND GRASS

◆ "Triton Cove," pieced by John Q. Adams; quilted by Angela Walters.

Triton Cove

FINISHED QUILT: 72½" x 80½"

I'm a big fan of fabric. A big, big fan. And, admittedly, many of my projects begin with the desire to cut into and use a particular fabric or fabric line. I tend to create blocks and quilt layouts that show off the prints, patterns, and textures of my favorite fabrics so the quilts become long-term ways for me to continue enjoying the fabric designs that I so love.

"Triton Cove" is yet another example of this. I decided it was time to finally cut into a long-held fabric collection—one that had been sitting on my shelf loved but unused for years—and make something that can be enjoyed in my home by me and my family.

Made simply from large squares and flying-geese units, the quilt provides movement and composition without sacrificing the beauty of the large-scale fabric designs. And rather than choosing a pure solid as the backdrop, I found a wonderful textured shot cotton that pulls in several different colors and tones from the prints.

My recommendation? Stop collecting and hoarding your favorite fabrics and make something from them instead. Like me, you'll find yourself with a new quilt that can be loved better than a stack of fat quarters.

MATERIALS

Yardage is based on 42"-wide fabric.

½ yard *each* of 12 assorted prints for flying-geese units and squares

3⅛ yards of gray-green shot cotton for flying-geese units and sashing*

⅔ yard of fabric for binding

5⅛ yards of fabric for backing

80" x 88" piece of batting

*A shot cotton uses one thread color for the warp and a different thread color for the weft, giving the fabric depth and visual interest. If you prefer, you can substitute a solid fabric.

CUTTING

From the gray-green shot cotton, cut:
13 strips, 4½" x 42"; cut into:
    25 rectangles, 4½" x 8½"
    50 squares, 4½" x 4½"
16 strips, 2½" x 42"

From the assorted prints, cut a *total* of:
45 squares, 8½" x 8½"
25 rectangles, 4½" x 8½"
50 squares, 4½" x 4½" (you'll need 25 pairs of 2 matching squares)

From the binding fabric, cut:
8 strips, 2½" x 42"

FLYING-GEESE UNITS

1. Draw a diagonal line from corner to corner on the wrong side of each gray-green square. Place a marked square on one end of a print rectangle, right sides together. Sew on the marked line. Trim the excess corner fabric, leaving a ¼" seam allowance, and press the resulting triangle open. Repeat the process on the other end of the rectangle to complete a flying-geese unit. Make a total of 25 units.

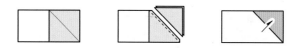

Make 25.

2. Repeat step 1, using two matching print squares and one gray-green rectangle. Make a total of 25 of these units.

Make 25.

QUILT-TOP ASSEMBLY

1. To make the sashing strips, join two gray-green 2½"-wide strips end to end to make a long strip. Press the seam allowances open. Make a total of eight long sashing strips. Trim each long strip to measure 80½" long.

2. Referring to the photo, left, and the quilt assembly diagram on page 51 for placement guidance, lay out the flying-geese units and print 8½" squares in seven columns as shown. Sew the units and squares together to make the columns. Press the seam allowances in the direction indicated (or toward the darker fabric).

3. Sew the block columns and eight long sashing strips together, alternating them as shown in the quilt assembly diagram. Press the seam allowances toward the sashing strips. Trim and square up the quilt top as needed.

FINISHING THE QUILT

For detailed instructions on finishing techniques, refer to ShopMartingale.com/HowtoQuilt.

1. Cut and piece the backing fabric so it is 6" to 8" larger than the quilt top. Layer the quilt top with batting and backing. Baste the layers together.

2. Hand or machine quilt as desired.

3. Square up the quilt sandwich.

4. Prepare and sew the binding to the quilt. Add a hanging sleeve, if desired, and a label.

Quilting details

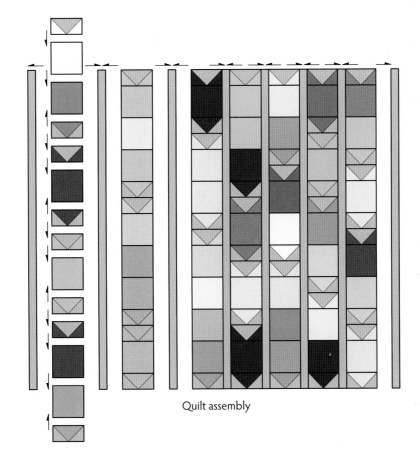

Quilt assembly

◆ "Fallen Timbers," pieced by Jenny Scheidt; quilted by Angela Walters.

Fallen Timbers

FINISHED QUILT: 64½" x 72½" ♦ FINISHED BLOCK: 8" x 12"

Here is another quilt that's a great choice when you want to showcase a favorite fabric line or collection of large-scale prints. I had made this quilt once before with a lighter background color, and I'm taken by how the choice of a bolder color can really change the look of the quilt. For this version, I chose a rich foliage-inspired green and the shade really allows the prints to pop. The best feature of the pattern, however, is the diagonal movement that is created by the repetition and placement of the triangles. And it's this movement that inspired the quilt's name, since it's reminiscent of both falling leaves and fallen trees on the forest floor.

MATERIALS

Yardage is based on 42"-wide fabric. Fat quarters measure 18" x 21".

16 fat quarters OR ½ yard *each* of 8 assorted prints for blocks*

2 yards of green solid for blocks

⅔ yard of fabric for binding

4½ yards of fabric for backing

72" x 80" piece of batting

* If you want a scrappier look, you can use scraps, at least 6½" x 12½", of 48 assorted fabrics.

CUTTING

From the assorted prints, cut a *total* of:
48 rectangles, 6½" x 12½"

From the green solid, cut:
16 strips, 1½" x 42"; cut into 96 strips, 1½" x 6½"
3 strips, 12½" x 42"; cut into 48 strips, 2½" x 12½"

From the binding fabric, cut:
8 strips, 2½" x 42"

BLOCK ASSEMBLY

1. In the top-left corner of a print rectangle, measure 4" in from the corner and make a light pencil mark. In the same corner, measure 4" down the left side and make a mark. Using a ruler, make a cut from mark to mark, as shown. Set aside the triangle for step 3.

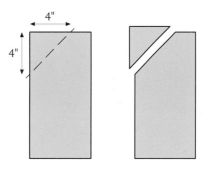

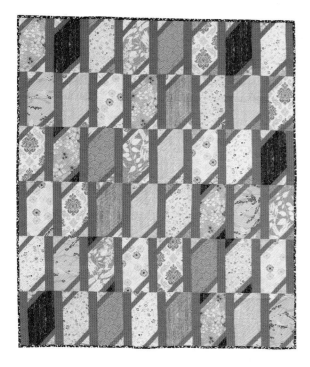

3. Lay out one trimmed rectangle, two green 1½" x 6½" strips, and two matching triangles from a different print, as shown. Join the pieces and press the seam allowances in the directions indicated. Make a total of 48 units.

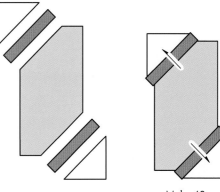

Make 48.

2. Repeat step 1, cutting a triangle from the bottom-right corner of the rectangle, as shown. Repeat the steps to trim all 48 rectangles. Set aside the triangles for the next step, keeping pairs of like triangles together.

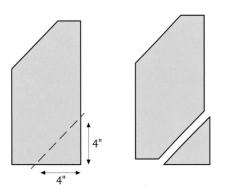

4. Trim the excess of the green strips and corner triangles even with the edges of the rectangles, as shown. The units should measure 6½" x 12½".

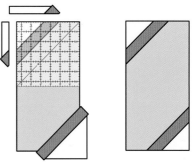

Make 48.

Time-Saving Tip

Stack and cut several blocks at a time; however, be sure to keep your pairs of matching cut-off triangles together.

Tools of the Trade

You can use any straight-edge ruler to trim the block. However, I found the task to be a lot easier by using my 6½" square ruler. It allowed me to simply line up the ruler with the corner of the print rectangle on each side of the block and trim the two sides.

5. Sew a green 2½" x 12½" strip to the right side of each unit to complete 48 blocks. Press the seam allowances toward the green strips.

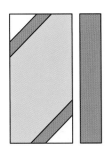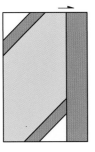

Make 48.

Alternate the Strips

If your prints are directional like the ones I used in this quilt, you will want to alternate the side to which you attach the strip. By doing so, you'll have 24 blocks with the green strip attached to the right side of the block and 24 blocks with it attached to the left. If your prints are not directional, you don't need to worry about this.

QUILT-TOP ASSEMBLY

1. Lay out the blocks in six rows of eight blocks each, distributing your prints and colors in an eye-pleasing way. The blocks in rows 1, 3, and 5 should be oriented with the green strip on the right side. The blocks in rows 2, 4, and 6 should be oriented with the green strip on the left.

2. When you are happy with the arrangement, sew the blocks together into rows. Press the seam allowances in opposite directions from row to row.

3. Join the rows to complete the quilt top. Press the seam allowances in one direction. Trim and square up the quilt top, as needed.

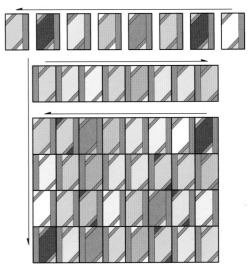

Quilt assembly

FINISHING THE QUILT

For detailed instructions on finishing techniques, refer to ShopMartingale.com/HowtoQuilt.

1. Cut and piece the backing fabric so it is 6" to 8" larger than the quilt top. Layer the quilt top with batting and backing. Baste the layers together.

2. Hand or machine quilt as desired.

3. Square up the quilt sandwich.

4. Prepare and sew the binding to the quilt. Add a hanging sleeve, if desired, and a label.

◆ "Cascadia," pieced by Jenn Nevitt; quilted by Angela Walters.

Cascadia

FINISHED QUILT: 70½" x 80½" ◆ **FINISHED BLOCK: 5" x 10"**

I originally envisioned this quilt as a slightly modern twist on a traditional patchwork quilt. Instead of squares, I built the pattern from rectangles. Instead of basic blocks, I inserted an architectural element of straight, solid strips in alternating blocks. And instead of sticking to the soft and creamy florals and "found" fabrics typically associated with a patchwork quilt, I opted for crisp and bold botanicals. When paired with a deep green to offset the prints, the quilt turned out to be a great piece with appeal across both gender and age divides. This quilt would feel just as home on a young boy's bed as it would across the couch in a modern urban apartment.

MATERIALS

Yardage is based on 42"-wide fabric.

⅝ yard *each* of 10 assorted prints for blocks

⅞ yard of dark-green solid for blocks

⅔ yard of fabric for binding

5¼ yards of fabric for backing

78" x 88" piece of batting

CUTTING

From the dark-green solid, cut:
16 strips, 1½" x 42"; cut *each* strip into
   7 rectangles, 1½" x 5½" (112 total)

From *each* of the assorted prints, cut:
3 strips, 5½" x 42"; cut *each* strip into:
   2 rectangles, 5½" x 10½" (60 total)
   2 rectangles, 4½" x 5½" (60 total)
   4 rectangles, 2½" x 5½" (120 total)

From the binding fabric, cut:
8 strips, 2½" x 42"

Save Cutting Time

To save time, fold each print strip in half and cut a single set of rectangles as shown.

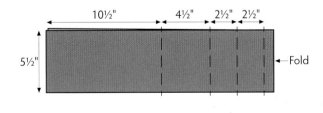

BLOCK ASSEMBLY

The quilt top is made up of pieced blocks and plain rectangles, laid out in an alternating pattern. For each block, you'll need one print 4½" x 5½" rectangle and two print 2½" x 5½" rectangles, all matching.

1. Lay out the matching rectangles and two dark-green solid rectangles as shown.

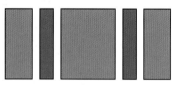

2. Join the rectangles to make one block. Press the seam allowances toward the dark-green rectangles. Make a total of 56 blocks. You'll have four print 4½" x 5½" rectangles and eight print 2½" x 5½" rectangles left over for future projects.

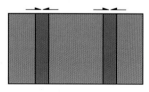

Make 56.

QUILT-TOP ASSEMBLY

Choose 56 of the print 5½" x 10½" rectangles; the four remaining rectangles can be added to your stash for future projects.

1. Lay out the blocks and print rectangles in 16 rows of seven blocks and rectangles, alternating them as shown in the quilt assembly diagram below.

2. Sew the blocks and rectangles together in rows. Press the seam allowances toward the rectangles. Sew the rows together to complete the quilt top. Press the seam allowances in one direction. Trim and square up the quilt top as needed.

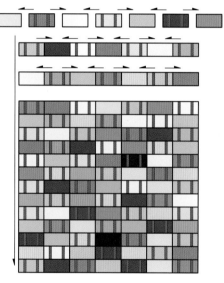

Quilt assembly

FINISHING THE QUILT

For detailed instructions on finishing techniques, refer to ShopMartingale.com/HowtoQuilt.

1. Cut and piece the backing fabric so it is 6" to 8" larger than the quilt top. Layer the quilt top with batting and backing. Baste the layers together.

2. Hand or machine quilt as desired.

3. Square up the quilt sandwich.

4. Prepare and sew the binding to the quilt. Add a hanging sleeve, if desired, and a label.

LAVA, CORAL, AND STONE

◆ "Glimmerglass," pieced by Kim Niedzwiecki; quilted by Angela Walters.

Glimmerglass

FINISHED QUILT: 62½" x 72½" ◆ FINISHED BLOCK: 10" x 12"

This pattern was originally featured in an early issue of Fat Quarterly, *the e-magazine that I started with some of my closest quilting friends around the world. For that issue, I made this quilt out of bright, child-friendly fabrics. I knew the design had much potential to take on different looks with different types of prints and fabrics, so I decided to make another one to include in this book.*

I matched one of my favorite collections of fauna-filled prints with a bright and textured red solid as the background, giving the quilt a whole new personality. There's something in this project for everyone—large blocks that can show off your favorite prints, Chinese coin–inspired columns that add a patchwork element, and easy-to-assemble blocks that won't try your patience as you work toward completing this quilt.

MATERIALS

Yardage is based on 42"-wide fabric.

1 square *each*, 12" x 12", of 18 assorted prints (or 2 yards *total*) for blocks

1¾ yards of red shot cotton for blocks*

18 assorted-print strips, 2½" x 42" (or 1¼ yards *total*), for coins

1¼ yards of light print for sashing

⅝ yard of fabric for binding

4½ yards of fabric for backing

70" x 80" piece of batting

*A shot cotton uses one thread color for the warp and a different thread color for the weft, giving the fabric depth and visual interest. If you prefer, you can substitute a solid fabric.

CUTTING

From the red shot cotton, cut:
7 strips, 3½" x 42"; cut into 72 squares, 3½" x 3½"
21 strips, 1½" x 42"; cut into:
    36 rectangles, 1½" x 10½"
    72 rectangles, 1½" x 4½"

From *each* of the 12" squares of assorted prints, cut:
1 rectangle, 8½" x 10½" (18 total)
2 rectangles, 1½" x 2½" (36 total)

From the light print, cut:
16 strips, 2½" x 42"

From the binding fabric, cut:
7 strips, 2½" x 42"

BLOCK ASSEMBLY

For each block, choose one print 8½" x 10½" rectangle and two print 1½" x 2½" rectangles, all matching.

1. Draw a diagonal line from corner to corner on the wrong side of four red squares. Place marked squares on diagonally opposite corners of a print 8½" x 10½" rectangle, right sides together. Sew on the marked line. Trim the excess corner fabric, leaving a ¼" seam allowance, and press the resulting triangles open.

2. Repeat step 1, sewing marked squares to the remaining two corners of the print rectangle to make a center unit.

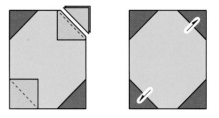

3. Sew red 1½" x 10½" rectangles to opposite sides of the center unit as shown. Press the seam allowances toward the rectangles.

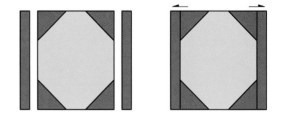

4. Sew two red 1½" x 4½" rectangles and one print 1½" x 2½" rectangle together, as shown. Press the seam allowances toward the center. Repeat to make a second pieced strip.

Make 2.

5. Sew the units from step 4 to the top and bottom of the unit from step 3 as shown to complete one block. Press the seam allowances toward the pieced strips. The block should measure 10½" x 12½". Repeat the steps to make a total of 18 blocks

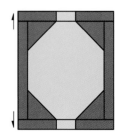

Make 18.

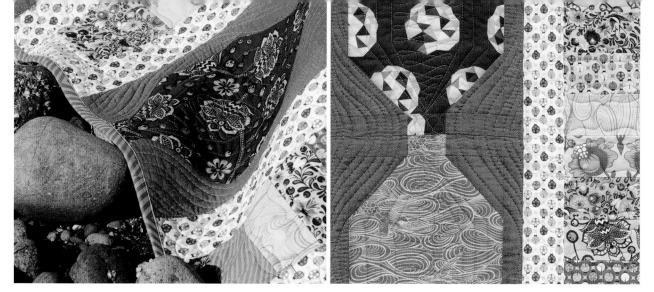

Quilting details

COIN-STRIP ASSEMBLY

1. Divide the print 2½"-wide strips into three groups of six strips each. Sew one group of six strips together along their long edges as shown. Press the seam allowances in one direction. Make a total of three strip sets. From the strip sets, cut 24 segments, 4½" wide.

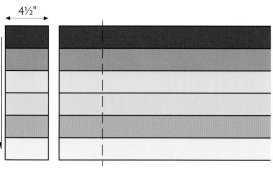

4½"

Make 3 strip sets.
Cut 24 segments.

2. Divide the segments from step 1 into four sets of six segments each. Arrange each set in an eye-pleasing order, making sure colors and prints are evenly distributed. Sew one set of segments together end to end to make a coin strip. Press the seam allowances in one direction. The strip should measure 4½" x 72½". Make a total of four coin strips.

Make 4.

QUILT-TOP ASSEMBLY

1. To make the sashing strips, join two light-print 2½"-wide strips end to end to make a long strip. Press the seam allowances open. Make a total of eight long strips. Trim each long strip to measure 72½" long.

Joining Strips

I joined my sashing strips using diagonal seams, similar to how binding strips are traditionally sewn together, because I think it makes the seams a little less noticeable. You can sew straight seams if you prefer.

2. Lay out three rows of six blocks each, distributing your prints and colors as desired. When you are pleased with the arrangement, join the blocks in rows. Press the seam allowances in one direction. Each row should measure 10½" x 72½".

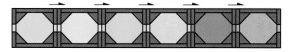

Make 3.

3. Lay out the sashing strips, coin strips, and block rows as shown in the quilt assembly diagram below. Join the strips and rows to complete the quilt top. Press the seam allowances toward the sashing strips. Trim and square up the quilt top as needed.

Distribute Seams

Make sure to alternate the placement of the seam on the sashing strips. Doing this will help make the seam less noticeable.

FINISHING THE QUILT

For detailed instructions on finishing techniques, refer to ShopMartingale.com/HowtoQuilt.

1. Cut and piece the backing fabric so it is 6" to 8" larger than the quilt top. Layer the quilt top with batting and backing. Baste the layers together.

2. Hand or machine quilt as desired.

3. Square up the quilt sandwich.

4. Prepare and sew the binding to the quilt. Add a hanging sleeve, if desired, and a label.

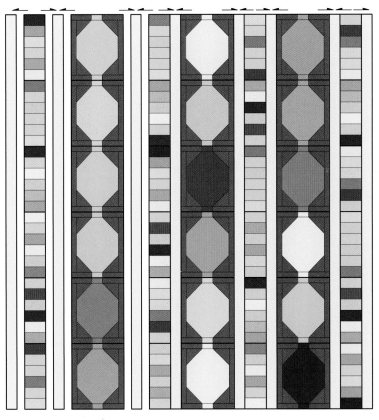

Quilt assembly

Pinnacles

FINISHED QUILT: 70½" x 76½" • FINISHED BLOCK: 6" x 12"

Of all of the quilts in this book, I think I was most excited to see this one come to life. From its inception on graph paper, through my selection of prints and tones, to its final construction, it was a joy to see my design idea realized. I have a strong appreciation for minimalist quilts, ones that are not overly complicated and allow you to enjoy them for their simplicity. This quilt was designed in that spirit.

Looking for a quilt with some masculine appeal? Something that's a breeze to put together? Something for the person in your life with a decidedly more modern aesthetic? Something to showcase that small bundle of favorite prints that you've been holding onto for that perfect pattern? Well, this project might be exactly what you're looking for.

MATERIALS

Yardage is based on 42"-wide fabric. Fat quarters measure 18" x 21".

4⅞ yards of gray solid for blocks, sashing, and border

6 fat quarters of assorted prints for blocks

⅔ yard of fabric for binding

5 yards of fabric for backing

78" x 84" piece of batting

CUTTING

From the gray solid, cut:*

2 strips, 18½" x 42"; cut 1 of the strips into 1 strip, 18½" x 29"

2 strips, 12½" x 42"; cut 1 of the strips into 1 strip, 12½" x 17"

3 strips, 4½" x 42"; cut 1 of the strips into:
    1 strip, 4½" x 17"
    1 strip, 4½" x 13"

5 strips, 7" x 42"; cut into 23 squares, 7" x 7"

2 strips, 6½" x 42"; cut into:
    2 strips, 6½" x 27"
    2 rectangles, 6½" x 12½"

6 strips, 2½" x 42"; cut into:
    18 strips, 2½" x 6½"
    46 squares, 2½" x 2½"

8 strips, 2½" x 42"; cut 2 of the strips into 6 strips, 2½" x 13"

From *each* assorted print, cut:

4 squares, 7" x 7" (24 total, 1 is extra)

From the binding fabric, cut:

8 strips, 2½" x 42"

*Cut the strips in the order listed. You may be able to use the leftover strips to cut some of the smaller pieces. Depending on how efficiently you use the wider strips, you may not need all the narrower strips listed.

◆ "Pinnacles," pieced by Cathy Reitan; quilted by Angela Walters.

BLOCK ASSEMBLY

1. Draw a diagonal line from corner to corner on the wrong side of a gray 7" square. Layer the marked square right sides together with a print 7" square and stitch ¼" from each side of the marked line.

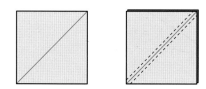

2. Cut the squares apart on the drawn line to create two half-square-triangle units. Press the seam allowances open. Make 46 half-square-triangle units. Trim each unit to measure 6½" square.

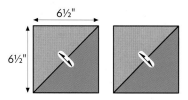

6½"

6½"

Make 46.

3. Draw a diagonal line from corner to corner on the wrong side of each 2½" gray square. Place a marked square on the print corner of a half-square-triangle unit, right sides together. Sew on the marked line. Trim the excess corner fabric, leaving a ¼" seam allowance, and press the seam allowances toward the resulting triangle. Make 46 of these units.

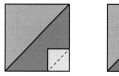

Make 46.

Controlling Directional Prints

If you're using directional prints, you'll find it helpful to arrange two half-square-triangle units with the print triangles in the center and the prints oriented in the same direction. Then place a marked square on the print corner of each unit and sew on the marked lines.

4. Lay out two matching units from step 3 as shown. Sew the units together and press the seam allowances open. The block should measure 6½" x 12½". Make a total of 23 blocks.

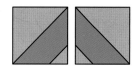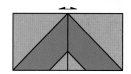

Make 23.

QUILT-TOP ASSEMBLY

You'll assemble the center of the quilt top in rows, from top to bottom, alternating between block rows and sashing strips.

1. Sew a gray 2½" x 42" strip and a gray 2½" x 13" strip together end to end to make a long sashing strip. Press the seam allowances open. Make a total of six long strips. Trim each strip to measure 54½" long.

2. To make the top row, sew the gray 6½" x 27" strips together end to end to make a pieced strip. Press the seam allowances open. Trim the strip to measure 42½" long. Then sew a block to the left end of the pieced strip as shown in the quilt assembly diagram below. Press the seam allowances toward the gray strip. The row should measure 54½" long.

3. Referring to the photo on page 66 and the quilt assembly diagram below, lay out the blocks, gray 6½" x 12½" rectangles, and gray 2½" x 6½" rectangles in six rows as shown. Join the pieces into rows. Press the seam allowances toward the sashing strips. Each row should measure 54½" long.

4. Sew the six long sashing strips from step 1 and the block rows from steps 2 and 3 together, alternating them as shown. Press the seam allowances toward the sashing strips. The quilt top should measure 54½" x 54½".

5. Sew gray 4½" x 42" and 4½" x 13" strips together end to end to make a 54½"-long strip. Press the seam allowances in one direction. Sew the strip to the bottom of the quilt center. Press the seam allowances toward the gray strip.

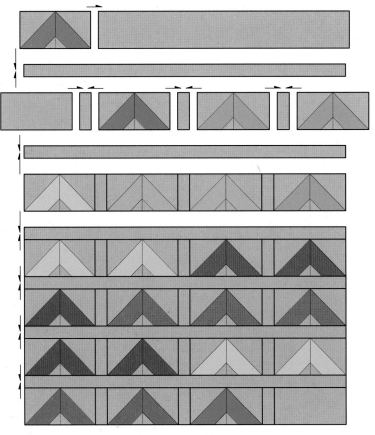

Quilt assembly

6. Sew gray 4½" x 42" and 4½" x 17" strips together end to end to make a 58½"-long strip. Press the seam allowances in one direction. Sew the strip to the right side of the quilt center. Press the seam allowances toward the gray strip.

7. Sew gray 12½" x 42" and 12½" x 17" strips together end to end to make a 58½"-long strip. Press the seam allowances in one direction. Sew the strip to the left side of the quilt center. Press the seam allowances toward the gray strip.

8. Sew gray 18½" x 42" and gray 18½" x 29" strips together end to end to make a 70½"-long strip. Press the seam allowances in one direction. Sew the strip to the top of the quilt center. Press the seam allowances toward the gray strip.

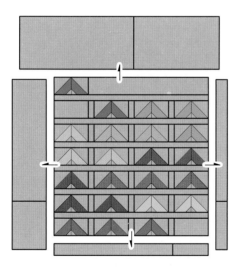

FINISHING THE QUILT

For detailed instructions on finishing techniques, refer to ShopMartingale.com/HowtoQuilt.

1. Cut and piece the backing fabric so it is 6" to 8" larger than the quilt top. Layer the quilt top with batting and backing. Baste the layers together.

2. Hand or machine quilt as desired.

3. Square up the quilt sandwich.

4. Prepare and sew the binding to the quilt. Add a hanging sleeve, if desired, and a label.

Quilting details

◆ "Fire Island," pieced by Daisy Mier Fredericks; quilted by Angela Walters.

Fire Island

 I really love making this quilt (I've made several). It's easy enough to be a pleasant project without too much frustration. The large pieces and simple design are very forgiving for those wanting to practice their techniques. The sharp-edged design is minimal enough to appeal to the modern aesthetic, though the vibe of the quilt can change with different selections of print and color. And the large picket-fence units that star in the quilt provide a substantial opportunity to feature your favorite fabrics.

Pulling from the colors and overall tone of the prints selected, I opted to use a red shot cotton as the background fabric for this quilt. I love how it simultaneously contrasts with and complements the prints, giving this quilt a completely different personality than if I had chosen a white or creamy neutral. It added the perfect element of fun and whimsy.

MATERIALS

Yardage is based on 42"-wide fabric. Fat quarters measure 18" x 21".

3⅝ yards of red shot cotton for background*

8 fat quarters of assorted prints for picket-fence units

⅔ yard of fabric for binding

5 yards of fabric for backing

76" x 84" piece of batting

*A shot cotton uses one thread color for the warp and a different thread color for the weft, giving the fabric depth and visual interest. If you prefer, you can substitute a solid fabric.

CUTTING

From the *lengthwise grain* of the red shot cotton, cut:
1 strip, 36" x 102"; cut the strip into:
    3 strips, 4½" x 68½"
    18 strips, 4½" x 32½"

From the *crosswise grain* of the red shot cotton, cut:
4 strips, 4½" x 42"; cut into 32 squares, 4½" x 4½"

From *each* assorted print, cut:
4 rectangles, 4½" x 16½" (32 total)

From the binding fabric, cut:
8 strips, 2½" x 42"

QUILT-TOP ASSEMBLY

1. Lightly draw a diagonal line from corner to corner on the wrong side of each red square. Place a marked square on one end of a print rectangle, right sides together. Sew on the marked line. Trim the excess corner fabric, leaving a ¼" seam allowance, and press the resulting triangle open. Make a total of 32 units.

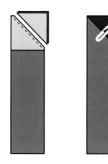

Make 32.

Sew Easy

If you want to eliminate marking a diagonal line, you can simply "eyeball" the diagonal line for stitching. Or you can fold the squares in half diagonally and crease them to mark the sewing line. Just make sure to sew a straight seam from corner to corner.

2. Randomly sew the units together into pairs as shown to make 16 eye-pleasing picket-fence units. Press the seam allowances open.

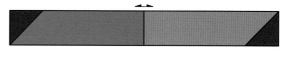

Make 16.

3. Join eight picket-fence units and nine red 4½" x 32½" strips to make a row, alternating the units and strips as shown in the quilt assembly diagram on page 73. Press the seam allowances toward the red strips. Repeat to make a second row.

4. Lay out the two pieced rows from step 3 and the red 4½" x 68½" strips, alternating them as shown in the quilt assembly diagram on page 73. Sew the rows and strips together to complete the quilt top. Press the seam allowances toward the red strips. Trim and square up the quilt top as needed.

FINISHING THE QUILT

For detailed instructions on finishing techniques, refer to ShopMartingale.com/HowtoQuilt.

1. Cut and piece the backing fabric so it is 6" to 8" larger than the quilt top. Layer the quilt top with batting and backing. Baste the layers together.

2. Hand or machine quilt as desired.

3. Square up the quilt sandwich.

4. Prepare and sew the binding to the quilt. Add a hanging sleeve, if desired, and a label.

Quilting details

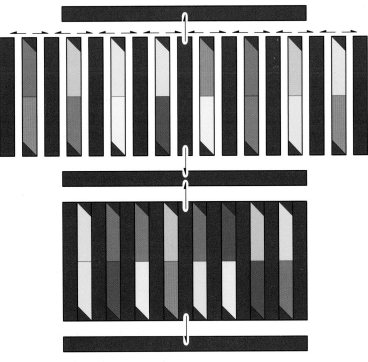

Quilt assembly

◆ "Big Thicket," pieced by Lucky Peterson; quilted by Angela Walters.

Big Thicket

FINISHED QUILT: 72½" x 80½" ◆ **FINISHED BLOCK: 8" x 12"**

Sometimes I really like to play with the building blocks of non-traditional quilt designs: big blocks, asymmetrical designs, off-kilter blocks and block placement, and improvisational piecing. But other times I like to take the more time-honored approach of building a quilt top from smaller pieces, repeating patterns to create something that, when assembled, has visual impact. This quilt was made in that spirit.

Composed of only two blocks—and two simple blocks to construct, at that—the alternating placement of pattern and structure add an element of geometry and architecture to this quilt. Is it chain links? Circuitry? A garden maze? A blueprint? That's up to the fabric to imply, and the viewer to decide.

For this project I used perhaps the most eclectic mix of prints and colors that I've ever pulled together. At first I was afraid of the bold and seemingly unrelated colors and patterns, but I came to love the collection after pairing it with a cool gray that helped temper the quilt's whimsical-gone-crazy feel.

MATERIALS

Yardage is based on 42"-wide fabric. Fat quarters measure 18" x 21".

15 fat quarters of assorted prints for blocks

3 yards of gray solid for blocks

⅔ yard of fabric for binding

5¼ yards of fabric for backing

80" x 88" piece of batting

CUTTING

From the gray solid, cut:
8 strips, 8½" x 42"; cut into 120 rectangles, 2½" x 8½"
2 strips, 12½" x 42"; cut into 30 rectangles, 2½" x 12½"

From the assorted prints, cut a *total* of:
30 rectangles, 4½" x 8½"
60 rectangles, 3½" x 12½" (30 sets of 2 matching rectangles)

From the binding fabric, cut:
8 strips, 2½" x 42"

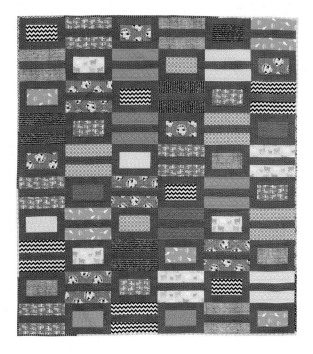

BLOCK ASSEMBLY

1. To make block A, sew gray 2½" x 8½" rectangles to the top and bottom of a print 4½" x 8½" rectangle. Press the seam allowances toward the gray rectangles. Sew gray 2½" x 8½" rectangles to opposite sides of the unit to complete the block. Press the seam allowances toward the gray rectangles. The block should measure 8½" x 12½". Make a total of 30 of block A.

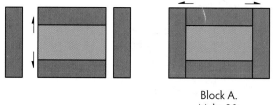

Block A.
Make 30.

Quick and Easy

Use chain piecing to quickly piece the blocks in this quilt.

2. To make block B, sew together two matching print 3½" x 12½" rectangles and one gray 2½" x 12½" rectangle as shown to make one block. Press the seam allowances toward the gray rectangle. The block should measure 8½" x 12½". Make a total of 30 of block B.

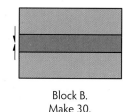

Block B.
Make 30.

QUILT-TOP ASSEMBLY

1. Lay out the blocks in 10 rows of six blocks each, alternating the A and B blocks as shown in the quilt assembly diagram on page 77 and distributing your prints and colors in an eye-pleasing way.

2. When you are pleased with the arrangement, join the blocks into rows. Press the seam allowances toward block A.

3. Join the rows and press the seam allowances in one direction. Trim and square up the quilt top as needed.

FINISHING THE QUILT

For detailed instructions on finishing techniques, refer to ShopMartingale.com/HowtoQuilt.

1. Cut and piece the backing fabric so it is 6" to 8" larger than the quilt top. Layer the quilt top with batting and backing. Baste the layers together.

2. Hand or machine quilt as desired.

3. Square up the quilt sandwich.

4. Prepare and sew the binding to the quilt. Add a hanging sleeve, if desired, and a label.

Quilting details

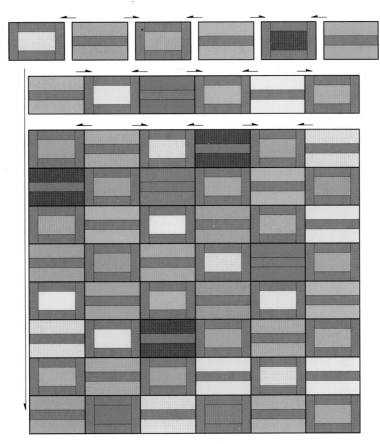

Quilt assembly

Acknowledgments

I would like to pass along my gratitude, love, and big bear hugs to the individuals and organizations whose support, generosity, and encouragement helped make this book a reality:

◆ To Lissa and the team at Moda Fabrics; Kimberly and the team at the Fat Quarter Shop; Michelle, Gina, and the team at Cloud 9 Fabrics; Anais, Pat, and the team at Art Gallery Fabrics; Cynthia and the team at Birch Fabrics; Christine and the team at Michael Miller Fabrics; and Jennifer, Kathy, and the team at Quilters Dream Batting.

◆ To designers extraordinaire, all-around awesome people, and my friends: Tula Pink and Alison Glass.

◆ To my most excellent pattern testers and piecers:
Meli (munchkinquilts.blogspot.com),
Kristen (kd-quilts.com),
Jenny (squawkthat.com),
Rebecca (restitcherator.blogspot.com),
Carol (sowingstitches.blogspot.com),
Rosanne (notafloralgirl.blogspot.co.uk),
Daisy (ldq.outlandishthreads.com),
Jenn (knitnlit.blogspot.com),
Lucky (imluckyquilts.blogspot.com),
and Kim (gogokim.blogspot.com).
I couldn't have done this without your help!

◆ To the *Fat Quarterly* team—Katy, Brioni, Tacha, and Lynne—and our extended family (Laura Jane, Lu, Mandy, and Justine), as well as to the ladies of the Sweet Hot Yams (Monica, Mo, Heather, Violet, Elizabeth, Traci, Kristin, Jen, Irene, and the gang) for being my own personal cheerleading section. I love you all.

◆ To the unstoppable force of nature known simply as Jaybird Quilts. Julie, thanks for always believing in me, pushing me in the right direction, and kicking me in the pants when I needed it.

◆ To Karen, Karen, Nancy, Mary, and the incredible team at Martingale for their never-ending patience with a very busy quilting dad. Special thanks to Cathy Reitan who went above and beyond the call of duty to help this book come together.

◆ To Angela Walters, of whose work I am in constant awe. You truly elevate everything you touch. I value our collaboration and look forward to continuing to work together.

◆ And finally, to the countless quilters and bloggers that have become my friends over the years, and whose bursts of creative inspiration, words of encouragement, and support always seem to come when I need it the most.

Happy sewing!

About the Author

JOHN Q. ADAMS is a father of three who enjoys sewing and quilting in his spare time. Inspired by the growing number of crafting blogs and the emergence of vibrant, modern fabrics in the quilting industry, John taught himself how to use a sewing machine in 2004 and hasn't looked back. He started his popular blog, QuiltDad.com, in 2008 to share his love of patchwork with others.

Since then, John has become very active in online quilting communities. Today, he applies his modern quilting aesthetic to designing original quilt patterns for both fabric designers and fabric companies, and he frequently contributes to creative blogs, books, and other collaborative endeavors. John is a published author and co-founder of the popular e-magazine and book series for modern quilters, *Fat Quarterly*.

John was born and raised in Brooklyn, New York, and currently lives in Holly Springs, North Carolina, with his family, which includes twin daughters, Megan and Bevin, and son, Sean. He earned his undergraduate and master's degrees at the University of North Carolina and, when he isn't sewing, enjoys cheering for the UNC Tar Heels.

What's your creative passion?

Find it at ShopMartingale.com

books • eBooks • ePatterns • daily blog • free projects
videos • tutorials • inspiration • giveaways

Martingale®
Create with Confidence

OKANAGAN REGIONAL LIBRARY
3 3132 03688 4973